Flipping History: How to Start Flipping Your Classroom Today

D1457215

Elizabeth Miller

DEDICATION

To all of the teachers in my life.

CONTENTS

ACKNOWLEDGMENTS

There are many people that I need to thank for their support of this project. First of all, thank you to my parents for your constant love and support. You instilled the value of education in me at an early age, and I would not be the teacher I am without you. Thank you to my friends for reading my blog when no one else would and for understanding that a $2.00 royalty check can feel like $1 million (and celebrating accordingly)! Thank you to my colleagues. Because of you, I truly love my job. Thank you to the #flipclass community for your constant inspiration! Finally, thank you to Doug for your enthusiasm for every crazy idea I come up with. I wish everyone could know what it is like to have someone who supports and believes in you unfailingly. I'm lucky to have so many wonderful people in my life.

1 INTRODUCTION

"I feel like I'm in Panera," said one of my students. I thought about it, and I had to agree...to a point. I'd love to offer them delicious hot cocoa and yummy pastries as they work on their projects. However, the school nurse would probably hunt me down faster than a missing laptop cart.

As soft jazz played, students lay strewn about the room working on independent projects. Some were sitting at desks grouped together; some sat in a "cubicle" in the back of the room, a quiet refuge from middle school chaos. Several were sprawled on the floor, while some sat on a rug near my bookshelf. Still others had pulled up a chair at the table I was sitting at. In other words, they were sitting where they were most comfortable and where they felt they could work most effectively.

And of course, there was the music.

A while back, completely by accident, I stumbled on music as an aid to learning. Because, on occasion, I listen to music while I work during my prep period, it was probably bound to happen. Like some students, it helps me focus and makes time spent doing tedious or arduous tasks go a little faster. One particular day, I forgot to turn the radio off before students entered the classroom and started working. It was the perfect complement to my flipped history class. We've never looked back.

As I stood to circulate the room, I couldn't help but feel cheery and peaceful. It's as if we all take a breath when class starts. We relax and simply start learning. It almost takes me back to days at the library in college just before finals. It was quiet but social. People stopping by your table, some in groups studying, others sitting solo. But the learning was palpable.

Education truly has an energy.

My classroom isn't always like this image I've shown you. Some days it's noisy and chaotic because we're making a mess learning. I like though that we have the ability to slow it down sometimes and spend some time learning to love learning. Flipping my classroom has given me this ability.

Perhaps, someday, I'll get permission from the nurse to have a "hot chocolate" day. Maybe I'll invest in some comfy reading chairs for students. For now, hearing a student tell me that my classroom reminds him of Panera, for all its humor, is actually a pretty positive statement. After all, people get a ton of work done there...don't they?

Flipping History

Why I flipped....

I've taught several grades ranging from 6th-11th, but my flipping journey started with my 7th graders. I teach just north of Boston and have a geeky obsession with technology. I'm always looking for ways to shift my classroom and have it be more student-centered. One night, I had been toying with how to go "paperless" in the classroom. While I was searching, I kept finding links to blogs on "flipping." Aside from real estate, I had never heard the term used before and became curious. This was a Friday night.

Cut to the following Sunday, and I had poured through every web page, scholarly article, and blog I could find about the subject. I became infatuated; my hunger for a student-centered classroom was finally being satiated. Flipping! What is it you ask? Well, it's simple really (and yet so complex in many ways). Flipping involves taking the traditional model of teaching and reversing it.

The traditional method of instruction involves giving direct instruction to students (usually in the form of a lecture) at school and having them complete some kind of reinforcement at home (usually a worksheet). Now I realize...not all traditional classes are as simplistic as this picture. I know that you're a dedicated teacher who has an engaging and amazing classroom. If you never flip your class, you will still be an amazing teacher delivering awesome lesson plans. Please don't think I am in any way saying that the flipped classroom is the end-all, be-all.

That being said, traditional classrooms tend to be, by nature, teacher-

centered. You deliver the content, students absorb it. As a history teacher, I am especially guilty of this habit. History as a curriculum area relies heavily on the lecture. There are, of course, plays, projects, and films. Those always seemed to be "extra" though. As in "if we get through this unit, we can watch this film" or "at the end of this unit this is the project I give."
I wanted to find a way for those extras to be the norm. Flipped classrooms do that. So what is a flipped classroom exactly?

In its most basic sense, a flipped classroom delivers direct content (usually via video) to students outside of school. The application part (projects, document analysis, and discussion) is then done in class. In a more complex sense, it shifts the room from "teacher-centered" to "student-centered". Students are now the curators of content and driving the discussion.

I knew I wanted to try this approach. I was itching to implement more technology into the course, and the idea of ridding myself of the lecture was freeing. Much of the research at the time focused on its use in math and science classrooms. Could it work for me in history? I was convinced it could and started the process of flipping my class. No waiting until next year; this change was going to happen now. That was in 2011.

Of course, once I stepped back I realized that it couldn't be such an immediate process. I had so many questions.

1. What kind of software should I use? What will work best for me? Should I tape myself lecturing, or lecture over my current PowerPoints with only voice? What will convert between my Mac at home and my PC at school? What if I look or sound like a total dork?

2. How will kids react to switching halfway through the year? Should I ease them in with one or two lectures this unit before fully flipping the next, is that enough prep?

3. How will parents react? Will they think I'm just being lazy? I'm not! I just want more individualized attention time for their kids.

4. How will administration react? I am constantly being told that our principal wants to shift away from lecture based classes, but how will it look when I'm walking around my class instead of standing in front of it? Will it seem like I'm lazy if I'm having student-driven projects?

5. What if the technology doesn't work? I have found many great websites that simply don't work on our servers. What if this turns out to not work

either?

6. Finally my biggest concern: what if the kids don't like it? What if they don't listen to the lectures? What if they lose interest? What if I fail to teach them anything? What will I do with all the class time I have now?

These were big concerns for me, and I'm sure they are for you too. As a result of starting a blog to document my journey, I'm constantly getting emails asking for advice, so I thought I would put it all in one place. I'm always excited to help other educators interested in this methodology. My goal is that, when you finish this book, you will be able to start flipping right away. There is no one right or wrong way to flip, and that's the beauty of it. Different teachers may have definitions and rules. But this is simply how I did it, and what worked for me. Although this is how I implemented it in my 7th grade history class, this could work for any subject area. I have since also flipped 8th grade and 9th grade U.S. History classes, so the method is transferable.

I will offer you some concrete ways to start your journey including:

- How to set up the course
- How to record your videos
- Where to house the videos you make
- What to do with your newly freed up class time

Don't be intimidated, if you want to do this, you can! There's a phrase that a lot of Yoga practitioners use: "start where you are." So I'm inviting you to start where *you* are, whether you've flipped a lesson or never heard of it in your life. Start where you are, and end up somewhere awesome!

To summarize:

What is a flipped classroom?

A flipped classroom delivers direct instruction (such as a lecture) at home via video. This frees up class time to apply the learning together.

Why did I flip? Why should you?

I wanted to create a more student-centered class. I also had a variety of levels and abilities within one room and wanted a way to differentiate content and activities for my students. Finally, I wanted to free up class time to learn, explore, and engage. I wanted one-on-one time with every student, every day. Flipping will allow you to utilize face-to-face time with students while having more impact, and it will move your classroom to a student-centered learning experience.

Who can flip their class?

Anyone. Let's get started!

2 ORGANIZATION AND SET UP

Part 1: At Home

How will content be divided?

For history teachers, this has long been a question regardless of whether you are flipping your classroom or not. Depending on your specific subject area, you could be covering a time span ranging one hundred years or even 65,000! Okay, slight exaggeration, but in Ancient Civilization for example, it's imperative for students to understand how Early Man not only develops but leads to the civilizations that we study. I mention this fact because, regardless of whether you are covering Ancient Rome or the Revolutionary War, you need to make sure that students have a firm grasp of what happened before. I liken this to the field of mathematics. You cannot teach complex mathematics if students do not understand basic operations. Likewise, you cannot expect your students to make broader contextual connections and understand complex historical relationships if you are presenting the information as isolated topics. There is a long running joke in our history department that students leave me having learned about the Fall of Rome and pick up on the eve of the Revolutionary War with no idea how they got there. I mean, call me crazy, but I think some majorly important stuff happened in between; the crusades, the age of exploration, and the colonization of America to name a few. It has been my own crusade to fix this issue so that my students enter 8th grade with at least some semblance of what happened between their history courses.

Why am I telling you all this? You know this already! I think as each year goes on and we get more ingrained and engaged in our "area of specialty," we forget about other eras in history. I'm just bringing it up as a reminder because one of the great benefits of the flipped classroom is the ability to manipulate time a little more. Since you are not a slave to the school bell, you can spend more time developing topics that you normally do not have time to get to in either your video lectures or in classwork with students. Therefore, when dividing your curriculum, I recommend leaving some space at the beginning and the end in order to give students a foundation and resolution. Personally, this allowed me to take some time at the end of the year to fill in the gaps students previously missed.

For me, the easiest way to set up my class was to do it topically. You may already do this approach in the traditional classroom setting. I'll explain how it works for me in terms of both the flip and my mastery-based grading. I will use my Ancient History course as an example, but you could do something similar with your own content, whatever time period that may be.

I started by looking at the textbook that was provided for my course. I personally do not like the textbook we use. Overall, I found it spent too much time on topics that I did not find important and very little time on some key concepts. The particular book that my course was assigned was written over 13 years ago which means, in addition to being out of date, it lacks connection to many of the overarching historical themes that have developed within the field. It's really meant to be used purely for content delivery and not to hone critical thinking skills. However, regardless of your feelings towards your class' text, it can be a good place to get a sense of the total amount of content you need to cover.

From my textbook I ascertained that we would be covering four major civilizations: Mesopotamia, Egypt, Greece, and Rome. I also knew we would have some minor civilizations we needed to cover, as well as a unit entitled Early Man. By dividing topically, I could build independent units for each civilization and then string them together with the smaller civilizations, always connecting them to each other.

Once I had a major topic decided, I wrote the number of "subtopics" I wanted to cover. Subtopics ranged from general historical overviews (Introduction to the Unit and Geography of Greece), to specific people (such as Alexander the Great), wars (such as the Persian Wars), and even concepts (contributions, art, daily life, etc). Each subtopic became a "video lecture" for the course. I then took the total number of video lectures and divided them evenly between the number of weeks I wanted to spend on a unit. For example, I traditionally spent 8 weeks covering Ancient Greece, I found I had 20 subtopics. Subtopics were important to me because it both cut down on the length of the lecture videos and allowed me to focus each lecture around a very specific concept. Some refer to this as "chunking," and in my personal experience, it has really allowed me to pinpoint what my students do and do not understand. After figuring out the total number of subtopics, I divided them between 7 weeks, which means that students would be assigned 3-4 lecture videos per week. This schedule seemed very reasonable to me. I left the 8th week of the unit as a "Wrap Up/Review" week.

I noticed that once the lectures were divided, natural "themes" for each week emerged. In week 3 of the Unit, for example, the lectures would be: An Overview of City-States, Athens, and Sparta. Therefore, this week emerged as one where we would learn not just about those city-states but how they interacted as a whole, and what types of government each city-state developed. It then made sense to have a debate between city-states and to hone in on comparing the different types of government. As you create your unit you will want to look for patterns in the assigned video lectures, those patterns can drive the activities you do in class, and I'm sure you already have some great activities that you currently utilize. On the next page is an example of how I divided my Ancient Greece Unit (it shows some project options which I will discuss later).

Week	Lectures to Master	In-Class Project Options
1	Intro Geography Minoans	Texture Map Legend of Terrain Places of Interest Model of a Ship Poster on Palace of Knossos
2	Mycenaeans Dark Ages Trojan War	Perform the Odyssey Read Iliad (Create Soundtrack) Journal Entries Trojan War Poster Compare Disney's *Hercules* (Paper)
3	City-States Athens Sparta	Class Debate (All) Design a Greek Home Poster on Weaponry Persuasive Letter
4	Persian Wars Delian League Decline of City-States	Research Boston Marathon Poster on Trireme 300- Legend vs Movie Create a Shield Delian L vs League of Nations
5	Religion Olympics Theatre	Facebook Project (All) Mythology History of Olympics Mount Olympus Masks Perform *Midas and Golden Touch*
6	Philosophy Science	Medical Practices 2 Astronomers Weight Change Socrates Great Teachers/Academy
7	Philip of Macedonia Alexander the Great End of Empire	Bucephalus report History of Alexandria Battle of Gaugamela Investigate PW
8	Wrap Up	Unit Project

While I chose to divide my class topically, you could divide it whichever way works for you. Look at how you already lecture. Do you cover certain years during each lecture? Then you may want to divide your content by time period. Maybe you are doing a unit on the Civil War. Rather than create lectures about individual people and events, maybe you want to break it down by year. Devote a week to 1861, and within that, have lectures for important laws, people, and events. Or maybe you want to have one longer lecture rather than three smaller lectures. It's truly up to you how you divide your content for the videos; there is no right or wrong way. I would just emphasize to do what works naturally for you. For example, I learned from trial and error that 7th graders can handle 3-4 ten minute long lectures per week. However, that number is unique to me and my students. Maybe you would rather do one lecture a week that is longer or one lecture each night that is shorter. Think about your students and their abilities as well as your comfort level with presenting material. If you try to do a total overhaul of how you present the material with regards to order and sequencing, you're going to feel overwhelmed and out of control. You need to create a course and a pace that works for you and your students.

Some other ways that you could divide content:

Thematically. Perhaps in teaching the American Revolution, you could have a unit devoted to what it means to be a British Colonist in North America and another devoted to what it means to be a Revolutionary. You could also have an overarching theme for the year. Maybe you want to have your class focus on women's experiences in history. Rather than just cover the Progressive Era, you could have each week's lectures cover the content through a women's history lens.

There can be a lot of creativity and freedom in designing your course and dividing your content. Just as there is in designing a traditional class, don't lose your creativity because you're changing the format of your class- embrace it!

On the next page is a sample worksheet you could use to help your organize your content. I recommend doing this sheet before you start to record any videos. Even if you're flipping halfway through a school year, coming up with a road map will keep you sane and allow you to present the information to students as if you have flipped your class for years.

Unit Name: _____

List of major topics I wish to cover (its OK to list too many):

List all Subtopics associated with Topics:

Now divide the total number of weeks you wish to spend on the unit by the number of subtopics that you have. That is how many lectures per week your students will watch.

_____/ _____

# of subtopics   **# of weeks**

From here you can divide them thematically, putting the lectures together that make the most sense.

I use Microsoft Word to create a table (like the one shown for Greece above) and to write out the weeks that the lectures will be covered. That way I can quickly glance down and see what is coming up.

Will you make your own videos?

This is a personal choice of course. A quick Google search will lead you to hundreds of videos about the topic you're covering. In fact, some of these videos will be by "experts," higher ups in the field of history, world renowned for their knowledge of the topic, so of course, your first thought would be to use these videos. Why would you want your students to watch your homemade lecture videos when they could watch a professional video made by an expert? Well, for one thing, it's an issue of credibility. There's nothing wrong with exposing students to videos made by experts in the field; in fact, I think that is one thing we as history teachers can improve on. Students often learn about famous scientists in science class and famous authors in language arts courses, but we rarely spend time talking about famous historians at the middle and secondary levels. This lacking content is a shame because exposing students to different "experts" with differing points of view can lead to some very important discussions on historical interpretation and debate. So in no way should you shy away from utilizing the flipped classroom to showcase some experts in the field. However, at the end of the day, you are the teacher, and your students want to believe that you are an expert as well (and you are)! Just as they trust you in the classroom to guide them to the right sources, they will also trust you in an online format as well. Again, you may feel differently about this idea in your own classroom, but I feel that creating your own videos is essential if you want students to "buy" in to this model. With my own students, I do a few "live" lectures in class, so that they can get used to my style, before I release them to the "interwebs."

If you do chose to make your own videos, the first thing you need to do is let go of any perfectionist tendencies that you have, especially if you are flipping midyear or going into your first year with this style of classroom. As teachers, we always want to put on a polished performance, but every good teacher knows the unexpected is bound to happen once in a while. Yet, the "show must go on." The same applies to creating videos. Do your best with them, but if you're creating them with a "one take" software, do not go crazy trying to make them perfect. You can always go back and rework them later, once you have a better sense of how your students are reacting to the content you're presenting.

Different teachers also create videos differently. Some record their live lectures. Many colleges have been using this method, and I must say, I have loved being able to "sit in" on classes from some of the most renowned professors in certain content areas. This method simply involves putting a camera in your class during a lecture and pressing record. If you do this, make sure you either video only yourself, or get permission from students and their parents before filming.

Many utilizing the flipped method record lectures on their computers. Some use infographics and cartoons. Still others use a whiteboard app to show what they are doing (I think this is most popular for math teachers). Some teachers show themselves on screen, others simply use only their voices. At first, the possibilities can seem overwhelming. I will share what I have done and what has worked for me, but again, it's up to you how you approach video creation (and if you approach it at all- more on that later- I keep saying that don't I? We're getting to everything in due time, I promise!).

Partially, because I had spent so much time creating PowerPoints for my class, and in part because I just didn't know where to start, I decided initially to simply record myself giving a voice over to my PowerPoints. I chose to use a screencasting software that showed my computer screen and recorded my voice. I won't tell you these were the most thrilling videos or lectures, but for the first unit for my students, it got the job done.

As time went on, I knew I wanted to add some more depth, so that I could really take advantage of the fact that students were viewing the lectures via computer screen. I kept my basic PowerPoints, but gathered a host of websites, YouTube clips, history shows, Google Earth, and all kinds of related resources. I began incorporating these into the video lectures, just as I would if I were showing students these things in class. The key for me was using a screencasting software, which meant that anything I opened in the window of my computer screen would be shown in the lecture. I really think you should "keep it real" when doing these lectures. In other words, you are not a fancy production company, and your students know this. I think if you present the content in a similar way to how you do in a face-to-face setting, the students appreciate it and understand it. Additionally, you're going to make mistakes. While I often restart and redo videos countless times, there is a point where you just need to produce the video and accept that you're going to make mistakes while you do it. You're human and your students will forgive you, just as they do in a live lecture. Now that I'm a year into the flip, I am going back and fixing many of my videos. But the first go around? Well, I had to let go of perfectionism.

Once you get the hang of it, you can take it to the next level. You can add in video pop-up quizzes. You can film in front of a green screen and add cool graphics. You can ditch the PowerPoints all together and talk. There are a lot of options, but start where you are.

Here are some helpful resources in terms of creating your own videos. There are many more out there, but these are the ones I have either used or come across frequently:

Screen-cast-o-matic (http://www.screencast-o-matic.com/): This website is a free screencasting software. It has been a life-saver for me (and a time-saver)! I did not have the money in my budget to purchase a fancy piece of screencasting software and came across this on a teacher resource chat page. It allows you up to 15 minutes of free recording. What I like about it is that it is simple to use; you literally click and record. Anything you open in the "box" gets recorded. I use a simple microphone plugged into the microphone jack on my computer, and it gets the job done. The downside is that it is "one-take recording." In other words, if you mess up and want to fix it, you have to redo the whole thing. Additionally, you can't add in fancy captions and other special effects like you can with more expensive software. It is simple and straightforward, but honestly if you're just starting out, this may be the place to do it.

Camtasia: A good overview video of Camtasia can be found here: http://www.techsmith.com/camtasia.html The cost can seem prohibitive, but I know a lot of "flippers" out there have found a lot of success with it and swear by it. It's still a screencast; however, it has more sophisticated tools to allow you to edit, do retakes on particular sections, and add in things like links and captions. You can also do a lot of work with split screens and adding quizzes. However, it's pricey, upwards of $200.00 last time I checked; therefore, I would recommend starting with something cheaper (unless your district already owns it or is willing to buy it) to make sure you like this format before dropping that kind of money. If you do see yourself flipping your class long term, then this is well worth the money. They have versions for both Mac and PC.

iPad Apps: Unfortunately, Apple has not come out with a really great screencasting app. I do not recommend purchasing the app *Display Recorder*, since it doesn't work and has been a source of much frustration for me. If you don't need to do a whole screenshot, but simply want a whiteboard to write on or you want to import your PowerPoints into an app, *Screenchomp*, *ExplainEverything* and *ShowEverything* are great. I personally like the ability to open up various windows within my lecture video, such as History.com and Discovery.com, which often have short informative clips that illustrate what I've been talking about during the lecture. It doesn't hurt to play around with these though, since they're very user-friendly. I did have trouble importing my presentations, but there are lots of helpful tips on the web for these apps, so I'm sure with more time, I could have figured it out. I dream of a day when Apple creates a true screencasting app. But we'll have to wait and see.

Will that be the only thing that students do at home?
Again, like everything else- this is up to you. Many teachers utilizing a flip have students simply watch the lectures at home with no other activities. Still other teachers use various methods to help students further understand the content (and to make sure that students really understood the video). Some teachers still give homework in addition to watching the videos, but others consider the videos homework. Some teachers give a quiz or have a questions sheet to ensure that students are following along with the video and understanding the content.

I knew for my class I wanted to maintain some of my "note taking training." For the last few years, I've been using "Two Column Notes" from the Keys to Literacy series. Essentially, they are scaffolded notes (similar to Cornell Notes if you or your school district use that program), and they allow me to adapt different levels of scaffolding to different students. As the year goes on, I scaffold less and less until they can take notes on their own. Now, at the high school level, this is probably not necessary, but since so much time is spent on state testing in public schools, I think skills such as note taking and highlighting are falling by the wayside. However, I still try my best to supplement some of it. So I've included some scaffolded note samples for you at the end of this book.

I also knew that many of my students would not really think about what they had watched without a little more prodding, so I developed a "Coursepack" where I put all the materials they would need for at-home lectures. Essentially, for each lecture, I have them take notes while watching it, answer a few review questions (or complete some other activity such as a map or open ended question), and create some flashcards. I have included a sample Coursepack at the end of this book, or you may download a PDF version from my website.

Other Activities at Home

Critical Reading: In addition to lecture work, each week students read an article at home from a source such as the *New York Times* or the *Smithsonian*. The article will be a modern issue related to whatever ancient events we're studying that week. The students complete a critical reading of this article that we can then use for in-class discussions.

It may seem like there is a lot involved for at-home work, but I have found it takes the same amount of time (or less) than traditional worksheet homework and is far more engaging and enriching.

On Paper: Creating the form on paper can be simple. You could either create a form on paper to hand out or have students answer the questions directly in their notebook. You could even put the prompts right in the video. Essentially, you want them to have a space to make notes on the video and their understanding of it. You can check these in class while they're working on another project, giving you a chance to see just what they're thinking.

Pros: Computer access is not an issue. Students who are reluctant to use the computer may be more apt to answer on paper. Also, they could keep all of their forms in one place to make studying easier.

17

Cons: Papers can be easily lost, and you don't always have a sense of the class's understanding until they're in school that day.

Google Forms: In the past, I've used Google Forms to create quizzes and summary pages. To do this, I created a "Form" where I made the questions "open response" questions. I then linked the form to a Google Spreadsheet.

Pros: This was a good initial option for me because student responses went directly to a spreadsheet. I was able to pull up an entire class and see exactly what each student had pulled as "important information" from the video. It gives me a good overview of where the class is at, and the form also makes checking the assignment relatively quick for me. Additionally, the form cannot be lost before being turned in and will always be available to print.

Cons: Students don't have access to the form once it's submitted. This would mean that I would have to print a form for a student if they needed a hard copy. If they needed to revise their form they would need to submit a whole new form rather than simply revise the one they had.

Edline: The past two years, I have used Edline to create an "Interactive Assignment" (IA) for my students.

Pros: Since I now house their videos on Edline, they are already in the program; therefore, it makes sense to have an embedded assignment as an extension of this resource. Additionally, students can create drafts, edit, revise, and resubmit their IA as many times as needed. On my end of things, I can email non-submitters and remind them, but I can also correct the forms right online and send feedback.

Cons: It is not always user-friendly. Occasionally, students will think they have submitted an IA when they've only submitted a draft. Additionally, I haven't found a way to export responses as a spreadsheet. This makes it harder to form overall assumptions about a class's understanding. Finally, students have no way of seeing if they submitted an IA or not when multiple submissions are allowed.

Quizzes: A quick quiz can be a great way to assess basic understanding. After each lecture, the students take a 5-10 question quiz online. These quizzes range from multiple-choice to fill-in-the-blank. Because the tests I give students are composed of open ended questions, I (unfortunately) need to expose them to a standardized testing style, multiple-choice questions. These quizzes are where I do it. They don't count for a "grade," rather students must complete the quiz at an 80% or better to have "mastered" it. They have to "master" all lecture quizzes to take the Mastery Test for a unit. More on this strategy can be found under Part IV: Grading and Assessment.

Pros: Students have an immediate idea of their understanding of a topic and have to revisit content they don't understand. It gives me a good sense of how quickly they're progressing through the material and really puts the onus on them to review and revisit content.

Cons: Of course with any online test, academic honesty is always a concern, as well as how accurately a quiz can really identify true student understanding.

Pop-ups/Callouts, Etc: With programs like Camtasia and other, more expensive software, teachers can add "pop quizzes" and "callouts" right into their lectures. These are essentially questions that pop up during the lecture and that a student must stop and answer. If you have the ability to implement these, it could be a great way to ensure students both watch the video and understand it.

There are a myriad of other activities students can do while they watch the videos, and in fact, videos should not be the sole focus of a flipped class, they are merely a way to deliver content to students in their own home.

I have chosen those activities to be completed at home, ultimately to ensure that students come in with content knowledge. This way, they can ask more meaningful questions and have a foundation for their in-class work. For some students, watching a video is never going to achieve that goal, so it is always important to have some flexibility in allowing students to access content in a way best suited to them. For information on where to house your videos skip to **Chapter 3: The Online Classroom.**

Part 2: At School

So here's the big unanswered question: you've moved your direct content to outside of school, you've filmed your lectures, and you've put everything in place. Now what do you do with all that time in school?

I feel like I'm repeating this over and over (because I am), but it's up to you! What you do with your students in class depends on the age group that you're teaching, the content you're covering, your state standards, and how long your class periods are. I'll tell you what works for me and what a few other teachers do, but the sky's the limit here. This is why you've flipped: to rid yourself of having students sitting in desks staring at you- get creative!

I chose to utilize my class time to complete projects. But I don't do it every week. Some weeks we have in class debates, watch documentaries, analyze primary source documents, or perform plays, but a lot of our time is spent researching and completing hands-on assignments. I'll go over how I approach projects and a few in-class activities I do to hopefully spark your interest, but you want to personalize whatever you do to your class:

Projects

I approach projects in three ways with my students: preassigned, menu board, and essential question exploration.

Preassigned: This is how I approached projects the first time I flipped a unit. I looked at the subtopics for the week and developed five projects based around those topics. I made sure to include a variety of projects each week, writing reports, creating models, giving a speech, etc. I created a rubric to go with each project. On Friday of each week, I gave students a paper where they could choose which project they wanted to work on for the following week. I did not allow them to pick the same "style" project two weeks in a row. If for example, they chose to write a report one week, they could not write a report the next week; they could make a model, or create a song, but not write a report. On Friday of each week, they presented their projects in small groups. I made sure that the prompt for each project included the objective that the students were trying to meet and detailed instructions about how to utilize their time to complete the project.

Pros: For students who had never had to do in-class projects before, it gave them a road map to create the project. They had a very clear idea of what was expected and what they needed to do to accomplish the task. I knew in advance what the students needed for materials and could anticipate which students would need assistance getting them. Because they were completing the projects in class, I was there to help them as needed. This took the "parent advantage" out of the class. What do I mean by that? Many students lack a computer at home. I can fix that: I can get them computer access, and we can figure it out. Some of my students lack something much more important. They lack a parent who is able to help them with projects. Someone to guide them, check things over, and offer support. This feature is a major benefit of the flipped classroom, and it allows me to fix that issue. All of my students can now complete projects with the same level of support from an adult.

Cons: It was a lot of work coming up with 35 distinct projects for a unit and the rubrics that go with them. I also felt that it took the "hard thinking" part out for my students. The projects were already developed, and they just needed to implement their designs. It was also a lot of correcting over the weekend (I had 94 students, so I was correcting nearly 100 projects each weekend on top of all of my other work). Finally, I'm not sure how much they were "learning" versus how much they were just satisfying the rubric.

I think for my first flipped unit, this approach was a good solution since I jumped into the flip halfway through the school year. They were still getting used to the new grading system as well as the change in how our class was set up, so designing their own projects may have been too much at first. I have since shifted the focus of my projects to being less about following a rubric and more about developing questions, researching and exploring, and then developing a way to present that information, which led to:

Essential Question Exploration

For this model, I took the state standards for my unit and rephrased each standard as an essential question. I then assigned the questions to the week where we would be covering that topic. It worked out to roughly 5 questions per week. At the start of the week, I had each student draw a question out of a hat. This process became their project foundation for the week.

Over the course of the week in class, students were to research and develop an "answer" to the question. They could present the answer in whatever way they saw fit. Some students created posters, some wrote essays, still some created videos. There was a general rubric with minimum requirements to ensure that everyone understood the minimum expected.

I had a few "project option cards" to help students if they were stuck coming up with an idea, but more often than not they were able to think up some fantastic ideas. This method puts a lot of onus on your students, and you may be afraid that they can't handle that level of "open-endedness." They can...I promise.

Just as with the preassigned projects, students had to present on Fridays. However, I did change things slightly. During the week, I encouraged them to sit with other students who had the same question as them. They could help each other with the research and generation of ideas, but at the end of the week their project was their own. On Friday, they had to sit with people who had a different project than them and discuss what their question was and how they answered it.

Pros: I saw immense creativity from my students. They really became enthusiastic. They would be so happy when they asked if they could draw a comic showing the Siege of Carthage, only to find out that they could! They embraced the idea of helping each other research, and it definitely became a quest for knowledge for many of them. I really think it helped some of my students to learn how to learn, as funny as that sounds. It also offered me a lot of "teachable moments" with regards to teaching students how to use databases as well as card catalogs and indexes.

Cons: Since students only answered one question each week, they only went in depth with one standard. They still learned about the others through the video lectures, but it is something to consider. Additionally, because students randomly drew their questions out of a hat, they weren't always going in depth about something they were passionate about. Finally, I was still correcting a LOT of projects on the weekend.

This experience led me to look for a method where students would be going in depth in a variety of topics. I wanted something where they had some autonomy of choice regarding the type of project that they completed but also ensured that they were meeting all of the standards. I also wanted to stagger the turn-in times, so that I didn't get 100 projects every Friday.

I turned to:

Choice Boards

Sometimes referred to as Menu Boards or Project Menus, Choice Boards are something I absolutely love. Best of all, there are many styles. For example, some Choice Boards look like a tic-tac-toe board. Students select three projects from the grid to form tic-tac-toe. Some look like an actual restaurant menu. They select a small project from "appetizers," a large project from "entrees," and another small project from "desserts." Some list projects with a range of point values and require students to mix and match projects until they get to 100.

There are entire books on this topic, so I won't go into it in too much depth. I did include a sample project menu at the end of the book if you're curious as to what they look like.

To address our previous issue of too many projects coming in at once and to cut down on all projects coming in at the same time, I decided to stagger due dates. Depending on the type of menu, students turned in projects as they finished them. I also had a self-checking rubric for them to fill out before anything was turned in. This strategy cut down on the number of projects that I was getting that were incomplete or needed to be fixed. I had a hard deadline that all projects were due by and recommended deadlines to keep students on track. For example, the unit may be eight weeks, so that is the total amount of time they have to complete the board. I would recommend though that they complete one project a week to stay on track. I also had "extra" projects for early finishers.

Pros: Students got to go in depth with topics that interested them and had some level of autonomy with regards to the type of project they picked. They had a clear road map of what they needed to do and were able to function very independently in class. This freed me up to walk around and help students as needed.

Cons: Students that struggled with time management could easily fall behind without a lot of prompting. Additionally, the room was often chaotic at times with students getting supplies, books, materials, and checking in with other students. I happen to enjoy the chaos, but you might not. Finally, project after project can sometimes get daunting and repetitive if not spaced out correctly.

Now I don't want you to get the idea that all we do are projects. I stated it before: I try to rotate between whole class work, independent work, and group work. I also started rotating my project styles. I now use all three mentioned above. Having different options allows me to really tailor the activities we're doing to my students.

Other things to do in class:

In-Class Field Trips

There are a few ways to approach doing in-class field trips. You could create a webquest where students visit the website of an important site and hunt for facts and images. Many places, however, actually have "in-class field trips" already created. These are videos where tour guides take students through the site just as they would if they were in person.

One thing I really like to do though is create my own! I live near Boston, so I'm lucky in that I have a ton of great historical sites close by, but I'm sure you do too. Go to that site and film yourself. Tell your students why it's important. Show them around, be corny, have a blast, show them how fun history is. Go home and use a simple editor like iMovie to create your video. Remember to get permission to film if you need to (most places will say "yes" if you are using it for education). You can then show students the video in class or assign it for at-home work as part of their lectures for the week. Pictures are great, but if you can't actually take students to a physical location, this is a great option!

Films

I'm not sure about you, but any time we watched a movie in school, it felt like a holiday. As history teachers, we're so lucky there are a plethora of fantastic films, documentaries, and shows covering historical topics. Prior to flipping, I always wished that I had more time to show films to my students. Now that I have my class time freed up, I don't feel bad taking a few days to show a movie. Sometimes, I'll show a "Hollywood" version of a historical event and then a documentary covering the same event and have students write a comparison. Sometimes, I have students film their own movies, and we watch them. The point is that you now have the time, and you don't have to feel guilty!

Plays

Go ahead, take a week to put on a play. There are some great historical plays available. I've had students perform the *Constitutional Convention, John Brown's Trial,* or *Julius Caesar.* Assign some kids to work on costumes, and some to work on props and staging. But get everyone involved at their level of comfort. Perform for other classes, parents, or the whole school. Trust me, the kids will get into it (I always worried that they would think they were "too cool"- they weren't). This can be a great learning experience, and I promise, they will remember a lot more than if you assigned a textbook reading.

In-Depth Document Analysis

I love Stanford's Reading Like a Historian program. It takes primary source documents and has students source and analyze them in a way that connects with what's going on in the world today. I definitely recommend checking them out. Working with primary source documents or doing any kind of document investigation can be a great way to give students a window into the past. They are a great way to break up projects and give students a whole new appreciation for historical events.

These are just a few examples of hundreds of possibilities. Do what works for you! Use what you already have!

What about early finishers?

You are always going to have a few students who are early finishers. I have a rule in my classroom: "you cannot be doing nothing." In other words, they need to plan their time not just so that they finish on time, but also so that they have enough to keep them busy. I've found that most students learn how long things take them and adapt fairly quickly. Of course, you're still going to have those students who complete things ahead of time. This time should be seen as an extra learning opportunity for them. How you approach this time is up to you, but here are some things I've done:

- Encourage them to review their work. I do this before anything else. If they've finished early and the work they turned in is not at 100%, they need to go back and rework things until it is.
- Make them an "expert." Allow them to circulate and help other students with their new expertise. This is good if they finish one class period ahead of schedule, though not recommended as a long-term solution.
- Offer "extra in-depth" information. I find many of my early finishers have an interest in a particular topic we're studying. I offer them use of my library of books to select something that interests them and use the time to learn as much as they can. As long as they are being productive and doing something in the realm of history, I think it's great to encourage their in-depth study of a particular topic.
- "Manipulatives." I have lots of flashcards (students also make flashcards) and fun history-themed games and puzzles. I encourage early finishers to pair up with one another and review flashcards or challenge each other to a game or puzzle.
- Give them a chance to help you design something for the classroom to showcase their work. I've found that having students design my bulletin boards or display cases gives them a real sense of ownership.
- Let them create a webquest. Ask them to curate the best websites related to your topic of study and create a "quest" for their classmates. Offer this quest as an option to other early finishers.

- At the start of the year, have everyone pick a topic (from any point in history) that interests them. Tell them this is their "personal project" and any time they find themselves with nothing to do, they should work on it. Present the personal projects at the end of the year.

You may be wondering if student's push back against "extra work" if they complete things early. The reality is that a few do but most don't! Make it the "norm" in your room that you always have to be doing something, and they will adapt. You can consider offering extra credit for these things; although I'll be honest, I haven't, and it hasn't been an issue. I really believe that if you can find something a child is interested in, they *will* pursue it. Allow them the time to learn about something that truly peaks their interest and you'll be surprised at how much they are willing to invest.

3 THE ONLINE CLASSROOM

Regardless of whether you are going to have a flipped classroom, a blended learning classroom, or a traditional classroom, you need a good Learning Management System (LMS). This system can simply be a place to house your videos, or it can be an all encompassing place where you can have quizzes, project turn-ins, and discussion threads. I've used many of them, and Schoology is my favorite, but I've included some different ones I've tried.

Edomodo: This one was the first LMS I used. It had a lot of great options, and the kids really liked the interface. It allowed me to set up quizzes, have discussion threads, and communicate and connect with students outside of school hours. I only switched from Edmodo because a coworker was using Schoology, and I fell in love with it. Otherwise, Edmodo is a great option for your class. Many of the teachers I connect with on Twitter swear by it.

Sophia: This one is a tutorial site. It will allow you to house your video tutorials and quizzes. If you're just looking for a place to house your videos online, this choice is a great options as you can organize them topically and set them up as a "course."

Schoology: What can I say? I love it. It reminds me of a mixture of Blackboard and Facebook. The user interface is very recognizable for the kids, and I like the way it's organized and set up. You can create courses and folders within those courses to house all of your materials. You can also create quizzes, discussion threads, and polls. Finally, the app is great, my students really found it helpful, and I found that they were much more likely to message me through the app than via email. I can't recommend this LMS enough. I've had past students come back and ask if I was still using it because they really liked it.

Edline: This LMS is the one that my district purchased. It allows teachers to create a landing page for each course, and you can add things like folders, videos, and quizzes to your page. You can link it up with your gradebook and email your entire class from the site. I know a lot of districts have used this one, so if yours does, you may want to start with it before putting in the effort to create usernames on Schoology or Edmodo. Overall, I don't find it as user-friendly as Schoology, and I don't love the interface. The app also needs some developing before it's able to allow students to successfully navigate their course online.

YouTube: You can always host your videos here if you don't need all the fancy features of an LMS. In fact, I recommend housing them here even if you do as students seem to be able to pull them up far easier on YouTube when using a mobile device. I do recommend that if you don't want the public to see your videos, you set them to "Unlisted." What this means is that students have to click a specific link to access the videos. I also recommend that if you're going to make your videos public, you disable the comments. I learned the hard way when a stranger posted an inappropriate (and factually incorrect) comment that my students saw.

4 GRADING AND ASSESSMENT

One of the most important decisions any teacher makes is how their class will be assessed. This importance is no different with the Flipped Classroom. As with many other aspects of the Flipped Classroom, there isn't one right or wrong way to assess. Many flipped educators are using the change in their course structure as an opportunity to try different forms of assessment in their rooms. This may work for you; it may not. I decided since I was changing everything anyway, it made sense to start fresh with a new grading policy. I'll outline a few below, but to be honest, I am constantly adapting, tweaking, and changing how I assess my students. At the end of the day, I want them to not only "know their stuff," but I want them to *want* to know more (I realize that sounds like a Cheap Trick song). In all seriousness though, I could care less about "grades," and I know many other educators feel the same way, but we have to do them. That's life (well, life in public education anyway). So let's find the way that works best for not just us but ultimately our students.

Traditional Grading

There's nothing wrong with traditional grading if it works for you and your students. There's also no reason it wouldn't work within the setup of a Flipped Classroom. Flipping your classroom and changing the entire structure of something you've been used to for some time can already be an enormous undertaking. No one will think less of you if you choose to leave your current grading in place. That's a fantastic aspect of the Flipped Class community- come as you are and take what you need (but please don't leave, we want you to stay and then share, share, share what you're doing with us)!

Mastery Based Grading (MBG)

This was one of the things that really drew me to the Flip. I knew that I could change to a mastery based grading in a traditional classroom, but I could never quite figure out the logistics of it (and by "logistics," let's be honest, I mean time). I only see my classes for 40 minutes per day. That time is barely enough time to get through the Persian Wars, let alone teach, reteach, test, and retest. Flipping has given me the time to do this. So what is MBG? How can you implement it?

Mastery Based Grading is a move away from "averages" and the traditional point grubbing game we play with students. MBG requires students to go back and relearn material while being able to demonstrate that they have mastered specific standards.

In this model, students are graded based on the number of units they master. Each term for me had between 4 and 5 Units. Mastery is considered an 80% or better. To master a unit, a student must complete all tests at an 80% or better. They also must complete all work in their coursepack associated with the unit. An example of how grading works is shown below:

If a student were to master:
4 units = A
3 units = B
2 units = C
1 unit = D

Mastery of Units counts for 50% of their overall grade. Grade breakdown would be as follows:
Mastery of Unit = 60%
Critical Readings and IL's = 10%
In-Class Weekly Projects = 20%
CE Quizzes/MLQs = 10%

Remember those quizzes they take at home after each lecture? They have to get an
80% or better on all of those within a unit to sit for a mastery test. They may take the
mastery test online when they're ready, or if they prefer, they may take a paper-
based one in class or after school. Most students prefer it online as there isn't any time

limit.

This outline is just one example of Mastery Grading. There are many ways to make it work, and the percentages are unique to myself and my students. I've used mastery off and on, depending on the group of students. Another method I like is real point value grading.

Real Point Value

This method of grading is fairly straightforward. You give everything a point value. For example you may have an exam worth 50 points or a project worth 100 points. When using this method, I gave a point value to "videos" by giving them the points after they completed the at-home work that accompanied the video (the quiz or the form).

Throughout the semester, students accumulate points. At the end of the semester, you simply divide the total number of points students earned by the total number of points available, and you have their "grade."

What I like about this particular method is that students always know where they stand. I give them a paper to keep track of their points on, and they can check where they stand at any time.

From my end, there's no need to weight categories since I'm weighting each assignment. I've noticed too, that by eliminating categories such as "tests" and "homework," it has forced students to look at everything as being equally important. In the past, I've had students blow off an assignment because they realized that it was only worth 10% of their total grade. With straight point value, everything is important because everything counts.

This strategy also make it easier to have "extra point" assignments for early finishers. I always allow students working on choice boards to do up to one extra project if they have completed things early.

Is this a perfect system? No, but it's worked well for my students. I encourage you to experiment and learn what is best for you and your students.

Portfolio Assessment

This one is a method that's newer to me, and I've been using at the high school level, though I think it could work with middle school as well. For this method, I took the state standards assigned to the units we were covering during a particular semester and used them to create learning benchmarks.

Students had to demonstrate their mastery of a certain benchmark to me by a certain date. They would have to provide 1-2 artifacts of their choice in their portfolio and then meet with me to explain how these artifacts showed understanding. At the end of the semester, they had to write a reflection piece about the artifacts and their growth throughout the semester.

I liked this approach because it gave me a lot of one-on-one discussion time with my students. I also felt it held them accountable for producing quality work they felt was worthy for their portfolio.

I did these assessments using actual paper portfolios that the kids could pull from the file cabinet whenever they needed to, but there are so many tools now to create digital portfolios. I think that would be my next step.

This grading approach is a more holistic one and could be difficult depending on the way your district has things set up. It could work for you though!

5 ADMINISTRATION AND PARENTAL ACCEPTANCE

When I first started flipping, it was a relatively new phenomena. My classroom that year was sort of separated from other teachers down a hallway, and I found that fact somewhat appropriate. I felt like I was part of an underground revolution. We were quietly disrupting education as we knew it. It was exciting, and I was lucky in the sense that my administration supported me right from the start. I know others were not as lucky.

Now it seems flipped classrooms are everywhere, and many schools are encouraging teachers to flip. That phenomena has not always been the case. I remember being very nervous that my administration was going to think that I was crazy. My coworkers thought I was some flower child with glitter and jazz music playing, and I had no idea how my first wave of parents would react.

As with everything, there's going to be some dissenters, but by and large, the feedback was supportive. There are two keys to this. One, you must stick your ground. You know what is best for your students. Be authoritative about this, but of course be open to improvement Two, you need to plan, plan, plan.

Administration Approval

Some feel it's better to ask for forgiveness than beg for permission. I'm usually one of those. I knew though that this was going to be something new to parents and that having administration on board was vital. I purposefully put this section after the planning portions of this book.

I recommend creating a plan for at least one unit before approaching administration. Think of it as if you were pitching an invention on the TV show Shark Tank. You wouldn't walk in not knowing any facts or figures, would you? Get some numbers, read some success stories, have this information ready to share should you be asked. Present a clear, concise plan of how you're going to introduce the course, handle parental concerns, and ensure that your students will still be meeting all of the standards. Then focus on the positives. Explain how you feel this approach will benefit your students and all of the things you plan to do with your now free class time. Finally, you may want to create a presentation or at least a handout to share. Offer to let your administration sit in on the class, have an open door policy, and assure them that you will be transparent in what you're doing.

If going straight to your principal is too nerve racking, try approaching a vice-principal or department head that you have a good rapport with. "Pitch" to them first to get some practice and feedback before going to the top. Get a feel from them about where your principal stands on blended learning and flipped classroom models. Offer to present the topic at the next staff meeting to other teachers who may be interested in trying it with you.

If you're really concerned administration may not support you, offer to flip for a certain amount of time. Ask if you can flip one unit to start and afterward, you can meet and assess its success or not. You could also offer to flip one course section. For example, if you teach two US II courses, offer to flip one and leave the other traditional as the control. You could also invite them to join the online classroom or discussion threads to see how students are responding.

Hopefully, you won't encounter any of these challenges. As I said before, many administrators are very supportive of flipped classrooms. In fact, some are even flipping their staff meetings! It may seem scary and intimidating at first. "New" can be nerve racking. With some understanding and patience on both sides, however, you should be able to flip with the support of your boss and peers. Soon, what was once new will be part of the norm.

Parental Support

Parents want what's best for their children. When you introduce something new like a flipped classroom, they may push back at first. This new approach may not be something they've heard of. Since they have no experience with it, they may initially reject it. Understand that they are not rejecting *you*, just change. Approach them the same way as you did your administration, armed with facts. Explain how this change will benefit their child, how they can be involved, and how excited you are for it. Your enthusiasm will be contagious. If you are flipping midyear, I strongly urge you to send a letter home. Keep the tone light. Approach it as an exciting announcement. Remember, <u>you are not asking their permission, but you still need their support</u>. Create a fact sheet for them and offer to let them sit in on a class. I actually created a Parent FAQ video that was very helpful in easing concerns. Finally, understand that it *will* get easier as they see their student coming home enthused about learning and mastering the material in meaningful ways.

To help make things easier, I also created a Visitor Guide to give to parents and administration who visited my room. The guide explained what a flipped class was and some of the frequent questions that came up. I had a few copies ready to hand people should they walk in. Again, the more information you give people, the more comfortable they will feel!

6 DEVELOPING A PLN

The last advice I have for anyone flipping their classroom (or honestly, any educator at all) is to develop a Personal Learning Network (PLN). There are so many educators from around the world sharing information and ideas, and you can learn so much from them! This is really how I learned the majority of the flipped classroom strategies in this book- connecting with my digital colleagues.

Pinterest, Facebook, and Google Plus are great places to meet and talk with other educators. I strongly urge you to sign up for Twitter. There are TONS and I mean TONS of educators on Twitter sharing things every minute of the day. Additionally, there are "chats" that take place regularly where you can connect.

The current flipped classroom "chat" takes place on Monday nights at 8 p.m EST. Simply log in to Twitter and search for #flipclass. There are moderators and great participants each week. Even if you don't feel comfortable "chatting," you can just follow along until you feel comfortable jumping in. From there on, any flipped classroom tweets should include #flipclass, and you will immediately be connecting with like-minded educators.

Some other great resources:

Learning network of other FC educators:
http://flippedclassroom.org/

Educator Blogs/Site:

Penny University Press and Educational Services
All of my published work and curriculum materials can be found here.
www.pennyuniversitypress.com

Liz of All Trades
my current blog with links to my old content (from
flippinghistory.blogspot.com):
http://www.lizofalltrades.com/my-blog

Flipping With Kirch
excellent resource for math flippers (but really everyone)::
http://flippingwithkirch.blogspot.com/

Really awesome video examples:
Tomasson and Morris flip the English Classroom:
http://www.morrisflipsenglish.com/

Twitter Chats:
www.twitter.com
#flipclass
#edchat
#engchat
#sschat
#spedchat
#mathchat
#flchat

Books:
Flip Your Classroom
Reach Every Student in Every Class Every Day
By Jonathan Bergmann and Aaron Sam

Flipping 2.0:
Practical Strategies for Flipping Your Class
By Jason Bretzmann

Conferences:
Flipcon
FlipconCan

7 THANK YOU

If you purchased this book and made it this far, I just want to thank you! I love connecting with other educators and talking flipped classroom.

Thank you for the countless emails, tweets, and messages. I hope that you found something of value in this book and that it's something that will be useful to you in your practice.

If there's anything I can do to help you, or any more advice I can offer, please reach out to me on my blog, lizofalltrades.com or via www.pennyuniversitypress.com. I am also available for workshops, keynote presentations and consultations. Please contact me at liz@pennyuniversitypress.com

Happy Flipping!

Elizabeth Miller

8 EXTRAS

As promised, here are some examples of things I talked about in the book. The following page shows an example of my Two-Column Notes. The links will bring to examples of my Coursepacks, Parent Letter, and Visitor Information Packet. I do have Coursepacks and the PowerPoints that they align with available at www.pennyuniversitypress.com.

Elizabeth Miller

The Social Sciences

History

- _____?
  - o the story of the world's people
    once _____ was developed
  - o before written history =
    _____

- _____
  - o how _____
    influenced settlements and the
    course of history

Economics

- Systems of _____$$
  - o how people make their_____
  - o agricultural vs. industrial
    countries
    - Agricultural = _____
    - Industrial = _____
  - o have vs. have-nots
  - o _____
    - GNP = _____
    _____

- _____ and _____
  - o how people's _____ affects
    the world
  - o culture = _____

Political Science

- _____ and civics
  - o how people _____
  - o how to be a good citizen

- Study of the _____ and
  development of man through the study
  of _____, _____, tools, etc.
- tries to explain _____

Link to Coursepack online:

http://flippinghistory.blogspot.com/2012/08/coursepack-video.html

Link to Parent Letter FAQ Video:

http://flippinghistory.blogspot.com/p/parent-faq-video.html

Link to Visitor Information Packet:

http://flippinghistory.blogspot.com/p/visitor-information.html

ABOUT THE AUTHOR

Elizabeth Miller is a high school history teacher and the founder of Penny University Press. She holds a Master of Fine Arts in Communication Studies and a Master of Education in Secondary Education. When not teaching or writing she enjoys traveling at every opportunity. She resides just outside Boston, Massachusetts.

CPSIA information can be obtained
at www.ICGtesting.com
Printed in the USA
LVOW13s1350200817
545694LV00011B/664/P